ALL EARS!
Scan this QR code on your smartphone or tablet for a free audio reading of this book!

Scan the code, hear the story!

Having trouble?
Visit www.hpgentileschi.com
for help!

For Christiana,
who I loved to have chats and cups of tea with.

H.P. Gentileschi Publishing House
Austin - Rome

www.hpgentileschi.com

I see a cat in my cup.

I see a cat and a
cake in my cup.

I see a carrot
in my cup.

I see a carrot and a cow in my cup.

I see a clock in my cup.

I see a clock and a
crocodile in my cup.

I see a car in my cup.

I see a car and a
candy in my cup.

I see a caterpillar crawling out of my cup!

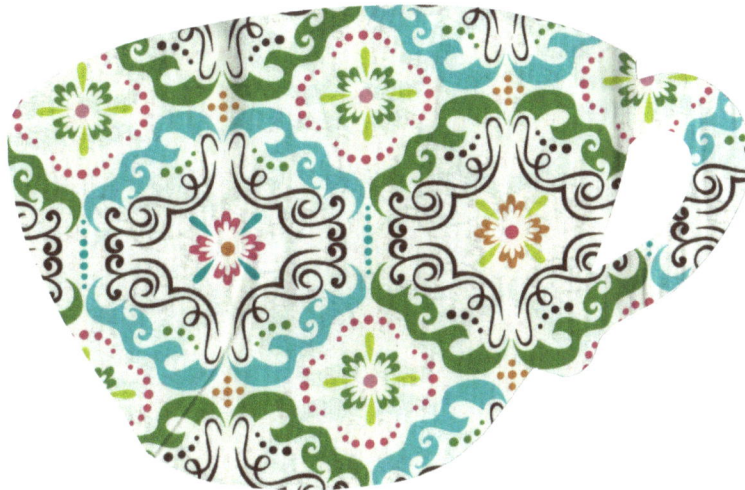

What "C" word can you
see in your cup?

C
words

cat

cake

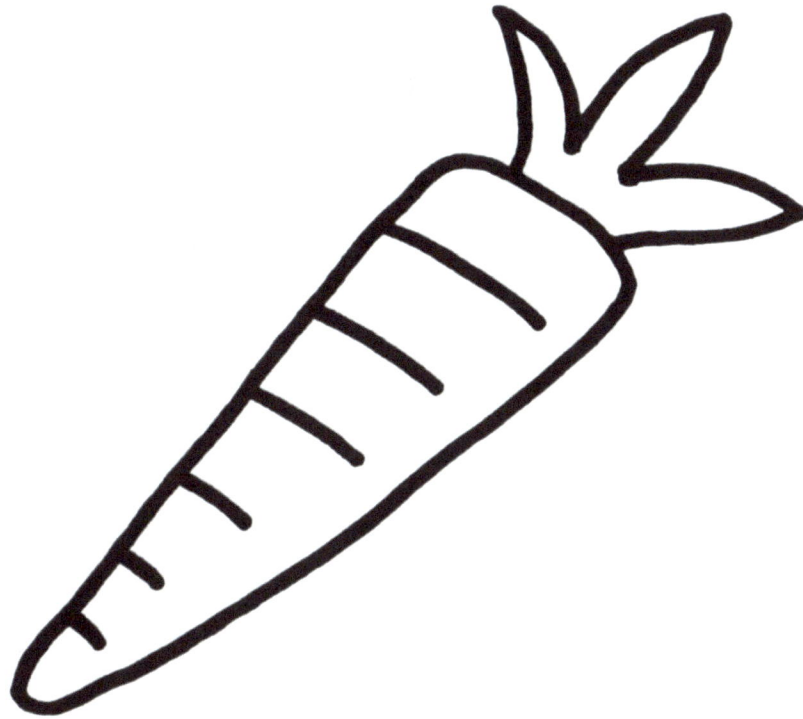

carrot

crocodile

car

clock

candy

cow

caterpillar

cup

C is for...

C is for CLOTH

C is for CARTOONS

C is for COLORS

C is for CRAYONS

Cloth Art

Make your own
Cat in a Cup!

Cut a cup out of colorful cloth and draw a cartoon cat with crayons inside!

I See a cat in my cup.

C

Pretend to drink from a cup
and say: "c, c, cup"

UDL and H.P. Gentileschi

At H.P. Gentileschi Publishing House, we create all our books and resources using the Universal Design for Learning (UDL) inclusive principle. The goal of UDL is to provide multiple means of teaching methods and materials to remove any barriers to learning and give all children equal opportunities to grow.

For this reason, you will find our books in numerous media forms:
- In print on paperback with easy-to-read fonts and not overly busy illustrations
- Digital eBooks on Amazon Kindle
- Audiobooks linked to each book with QR codes

Our books also come with fun experiential learning activities, such as Letter Actions and craft projects that provide physical movement options that reinforce the book's teaching objectives.

These UDL resources can be helpful for all kids, including English Language Learners and kids with diverse learning and attention abilities. Our book and curriculum characters represent the beautiful diversity that is found in our world, so every child feels included.

AlphaBOX Book Series

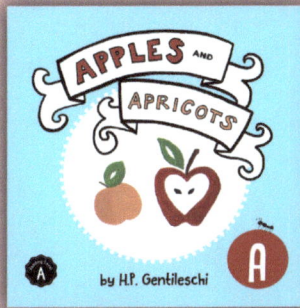

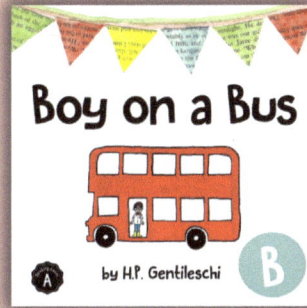

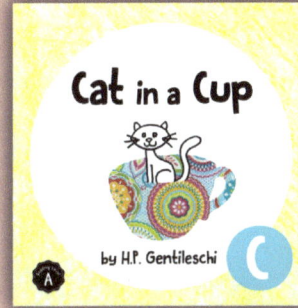

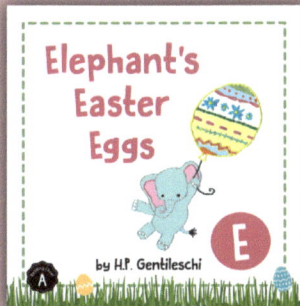

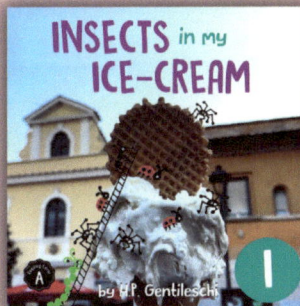

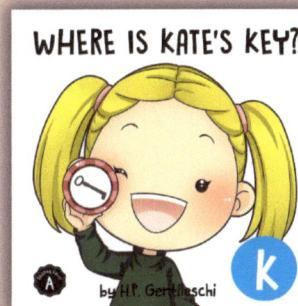

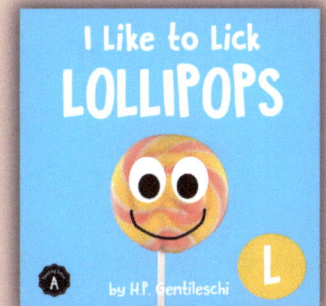

Apples and Apricots by H.P. Gentileschi — A

Boy on a Bus by H.P. Gentileschi — B

Cat in a Cup by H.P. Gentileschi — C

Duck's Days by H.P. Gentileschi — D

Elephant's Easter Eggs by H.P. Gentileschi — E

Is This a Fish? by H.P. Gentileschi — F

Gorillas Like Gum by H.P. Gentileschi — G

This Hand by H.P. Gentileschi — H

Insects in my Ice-Cream by H.P. Gentileschi — I

When Do You Drink Juice? by H.P. Gentileschi — J

Where is Kate's Key? by H.P. Gentileschi — K

I Like to Lick Lollipops by H.P. Gentileschi — L

MILK in My Mailbox
by H.P. Gentileschi
A — M

Does a nut have a nose?
by H.P. Gentileschi
A — N

ONE OCTOPUS in the OLIVE TREE
by H.P. Gentileschi
A — O

Penguin's Paper Plane
by H.P. Gentileschi
A — P

The Queen's Question
by H.P. Gentileschi
C — Q

Rabbit's Rainbow in Rome
D — R

Snake's Snacks
by H.P. Gentileschi
A — S

Does a Tomato Have Teeth?
by H.P. Gentileschi
B — T

Under My Umbrella
by H.P. Gentileschi
A — U

Victoria's Violin
by H.P. Gentileschi
B — V

The Whale in the Water
by H.P. Gentileschi
C — W

Fox has a Box
by H.P. Gentileschi
A — X

Your Yellow Yo-Yo
by H.P. Gentileschi
A — Y

Zero Zebras in the ZOO!
by H.P. Gentileschi
B — Z

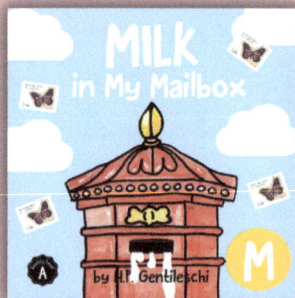

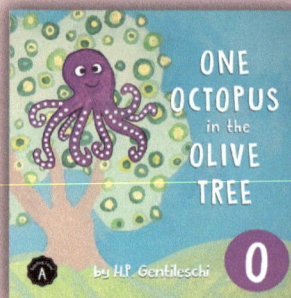

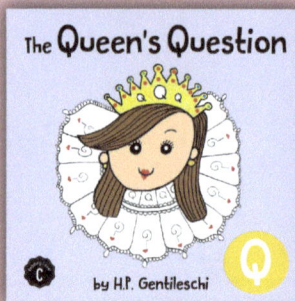

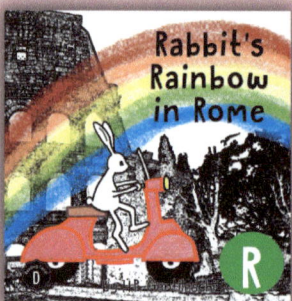

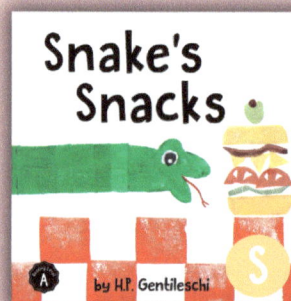

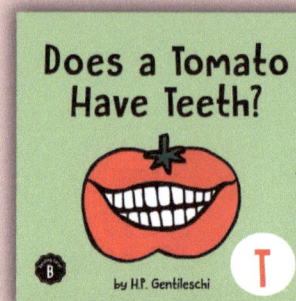

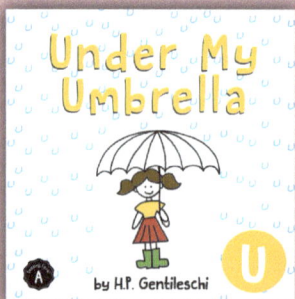

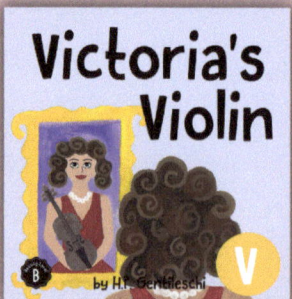

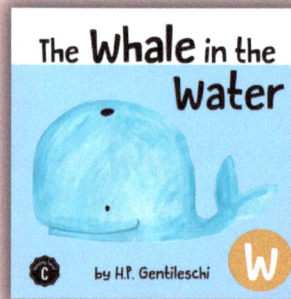

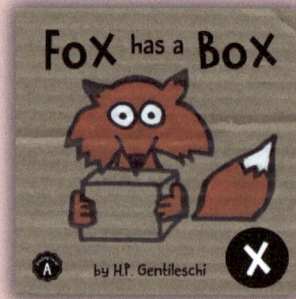

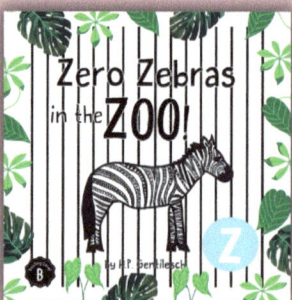

H.P. Gentileschi Publishing House
www.HPgentileschi.com

For all of our Letter Names actions, visit our website!
www.hpgentileschi.com

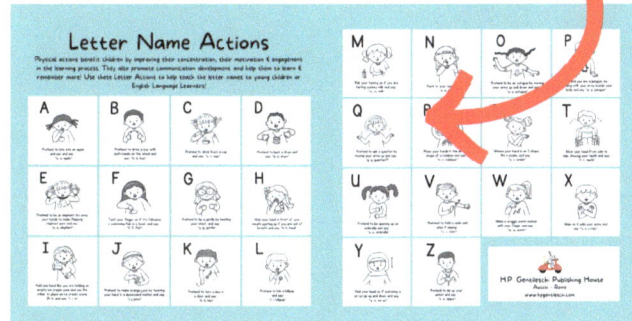

Educators and librarians, for a variety of teaching tools, visit www.hpgentileschi.com

For more engaging activities, teaching resources and to learn more about AlphaBOX books, follow H.P. Gentileschi Publishing House on:

www.hpgentileschi.com

We'd love to see how you're using the AlphaBOX series!

Share and tag your photos using: #alphaboxbooks

www.ingramcontent.com/pod-product-compliance
Lightning Source LLC
Chambersburg PA
CBHW041559040426

42447CB00002B/235